Washed Away

-a collection of fragments

Shiksha Dheda

abuddhapress@yahoo.com

©™®

ISBN: 9798524523471

Dedication:

This pandemic has painfully highlighted

- on a personal, social and global scale -

what we have lost,

what we still have,

what we hope for

and what we hold on to.

This is a declaration of that

Foreword

Arthur Schopenhauer once said: "After your death you will be what you were before your birth".

When we think of birth, we tend to forget death. The joy of seeing new life - the prospect of new beginnings and opportunities are seldom marred by the inevitability of the end. Yet, the possibility of death [the end] is ever-looming- that which is born, must die.

However, that which has died (or ended), will in some form or another be born once more. Energy cannot be created or destroyed; it is simply transferred or transformed. This collection serves to depict this cycle, namely in the context of my mental illness.

I want the reader to join me on my journey: why I feel the disorder galloped into existence, how this disorder has been sustained and how I view the future living alongside this disorder.

The collection has fittingly been fragmented into three sections. The first being the onset (or rather, remembrance) of the disorder(s). Here, I discuss how I feel I've battled through certain circumstances but have ultimately succumbed to them. I discuss symptoms or instances of the early onset of this disorder. At points, it feels as though this disorder was an almost inevitable destination.

The sections of this collection have been likened to the action(s) of washing one's hands. This is in part due to the COVID-19 pandemic (and the emphasis on washing hands therein), as well as being the main compulsion that I default to.

The first section - having its focus on the beginning/onset/reasoning of the disorder(s) - has been likened to the initial action of handwashing i.e. lathering up one's hands with soap.

The journey then continues to how the disorder(s) persists. This section touches on gaining a deeper understanding of the disorder(s). I also discuss handling the disorder(s) during the pandemic.

This section is likened to the second action of handwashing; rinsing one's hands. It is larger (albeit marginally), then the other two sections, as it focuses on how a disorder is continually fed by conflicting thoughts and circumstances. Further, as this remains an ongoing struggle, it is the most relevant section.

Lastly, as we reach the end of our journey together, we reach a conflicting amalgamation of ideas. On one hand, this is a hopeful section, whilst on the other hand, it is rather sceptical and hopeless. I want uncertainty to be emphasised here; the uncertainty of living with a mental disorder and the uncertainty of life in general.

This section has been likened to the final act of handwashing, namely drying. The intention of including contradictory poems in this section is to depict the continuous cycle that Birth and Death [the Beginning and the Ending] share.

This collection of fragments (little distressed nuggets from my mind), depict the physical and metaphysical struggle experienced with Obsessive Compulsive Disorder (and depression).

Every day, it is as though my personality is being eroded [washed away] by these disorder(s); I have to heal [rebuild/regrow] from the wounds or gaps that it leaves in my life.

Join me as I try to salvage that which survives; that which persists – refusing to accept defeat.

Part One – Soap Lathering

Void

I suppose I was trying to fill the void left
by living
by dying.

Is the door locked?

Checking the locked doors once.
Washing the dirty dishes.
Checking the locked doors once again.
Washing the linen.
Washing the linen once again.
Washing the dishes once again.

Checking to see if the windows are shut.
Checking to see if the taps are closed.
Checking to see if the windows are shut.
Checking to see if the taps are closed.
Checking the locked doors.

Counting the steps from one room to the next.
1.
2.
3.
4.
5.
6.
Is the door locked?
Oh no! I must count again.
1.
2.
3.
Are the windows shut closed? Completely closed?
1.
2.
I am sure that I locked the door.
1.
Let me check once again.

Checking the locked doors once.
Checking the locked doors once again.

Home

If people were homes; I have only lived in ruins.
Built from beehives whispered in my ears,
created by hornets' nests burrowed in my hands,
yearningly, achingly wishing myself away.

Why am I, mother?

When a baby is in the womb and the mother gets hurt, it sends stem cells to heal
the mother.
Why then does it seem like I'm hurting you now, mother?
Why can't you see me, mother?

I have heard your heartbeats from the inside
-    synchronised my breathing to its rhythm.

Why can't you understand me, mother?

If only we could abort the living
- if only I could wish myself
      -    wash myself away.

Sever the umbilical cord that binds us, still.

Let my veins bleed free.
Let them bleed dry.
Let me be cleansed of my lineage.

I am standing on the threshold of sanity, mother

It should be raining
      -    storming,
but it isn't.

I am standing on the outskirts of normalcy, mother
with invisible rain drenching my face.

Who am I, mother?
Who?

I am not you.
I am not me.

I can't recognize myself anymore.
So, then I must ask, mother.

Why am I, mother?
Why?

Lonely

Think I fell in love with the feeling of

being lonely

Fruits of the Tree

Waiting.

Waiting alone.

For just a few fruits

to fall into my barren lap,

with the deadness and promise

of once ripe life. Too afraid to climb

upon the daunting bushy green height once more.

The same height that many want to reach the top of.

Looking helplessly at the air above me, I still taste blood

-in my mouth-

-nursing a wound-

from an old fall

in pursuit of

fruit.

Ceaselessly

Pushing.

Ceaselessly.

Paddling
-     with all my strength -
-     in the bosom of heat -
-     in the lap of cold   -

I push on.

Looking for something better,
    hoping for something worthwhile
          I dive into the ocean of dreams.
          Seeing the horizon
      even further away
    than it was yesterday.

Not knowing
that there is no
shore at all.

I push on.

Ceaselessly.

Pointlessly.

Shore

You keep me at sea;
never let me walk upon the stable
earth of man.

I wander
from land to land,
meeting and leaving innumerable people;
yet I cannot find the shore that I seek.

You prohibit me from throwing down my anchor,
from settling down; unlike
so many others that have come before me.
And that will come after I am gone.

You give me no direction
-no clue-
-no guidance.

Just like the vast mass of endless water,
are the many intangible pieces
of the puzzling questions,
I have to ask you.

How was I to know?
That to reach your shore,
I would have to drown first.

The lotus

Rising steadily. Determined. Motivated. Headstrong. Stubborn.
Exploding into layers of colourful
beauty; folds of delightful
brightness. Coming
from a
filthy
muck
-obstinate
to leave-
forced
to
return.

Forever.

Martyr

I remember the war
-    intense, bloody   -
I fought for what I thought was right.
Fought for what I thought would make a better country;
a better home.
For me.
For all of us.
For you.

Wanting to be courageous,
reluctantly so at points,

wanting to carry you;
even if I had to bear you
upon my own weary back,

I thought we had won the war.
I thought it would be worth it
at the end.

Stumbling back home,
I see the native flag.

Torn.
Battered.

I see my home.
Torn (apart).
Divided.

I see you.

Embarrassed
-    by my wounds -
-    my scars.

I cannot bear your silence
-    your reluctance –
-    your evading line of
     vision - .

your disdain;
your shame.

I yearn now for the sound of bullets,
long for the uncertainty of spontaneous explosions,
thirst for the imminent possibility
of mangled death.

The opportunity to die a martyr.
A celebrated hero,
not live
as a burden.

Fighting
-     daily-
-     embattled-
-     at war -
within me.

Against this *civil* society.

Against you.

Against myself.

Shadow

Irrespective of where I stood,
the shadow of my personality always
seemed to mar their brightness.
I retreated to the darkness instead.
I retreated to the darkness instead.

Gone fishing

I was fishing for answers
-    in the murky waters of depression.

All the fish of meaning
I extracted
looked emaciated
and weak.

I put them back into the pond,
hoping that one day,

when I looked for answers again,
they would come swimming, again.

They would come for my bait of questions
-    being fatter and older;
more useful now,
more nourishing and filling.

Sufficient for the void that the hunger
of my questions
have created.

Heart(less)

It felt as though someone was ripping my heart
-      straight out of my chest.
Every single night.
Only to haphazardly put it back.

Always in the wrong way.

The find

I do not know how it started.

On Monday, the glass just seemed a little dirtier than usual.

On Tuesday, the speck of dust on the carpet appeared to be slightly
larger than it had been the day before.

On Wednesday, the photographs hanging on the wall in the
drawing room seemed a little less straight than it had on Tuesday.

On Thursday, all the curtains that had any red colour were altered because
everyone knows that red equals blood and blood is always bad.

On Friday, I steamed and bleached down all the cutlery and crockery at home
before I could use those filthy things again.

On Saturday, all my laundry was washed thrice at 95 degrees Celsius and were
made to dry indoors,
as the air outside must be unhealthy and dangerous.

And on Sunday, well Sunday was peaceful, a conventional day for rest
-      but wait...what is this I see?

All the days of the week have been engraved on my hands in the
form of tiny red cracks and spots:
guess I just have to wash them out now.

And who knows? Maybe I will wash so hard and for so long a time that
I might just find some relief.
Some peace.

The warrior

Setting out to win the battle,
I leave along with me,
myself and I.

The fight is vigorous and brutal.
I lash back with violence;
retaliate with anger.

I fight alongside myself,
against myself, with myself,
for myself and inside of myself.

The battlefield is appalling
-    my blood is spilled.
All my energy wasted.

Ill-fate is inevitable
as irony rides around the arena
like a fierce stallion.

I alone am the victor.
I alone am the
loser.

Fungi

One becomes two.
Two becomes four.

Afraid to allow
an open wound
to be exposed to
the air outside,

rushing to a basin,
I soak my hands in
a thick soapy
foam.

Washing.
Scrubbing.

Two minutes.

Waiting for the
voices

to quieten,
I continue.

Washing and scrubbing to
block them out.

Washing.
Scrubbing.

Two minutes.

Ten minutes.

Thirty minutes.

My hands burning.
Gentle stinging.
Now on fire.

Ten fingers;
palms covered,
bruises everywhere,
all exposed to dirt
now.

Only the cuts block out the voices.

Voices forever whispering
    -        voices that *scream*
when I see dirt.

I am okay

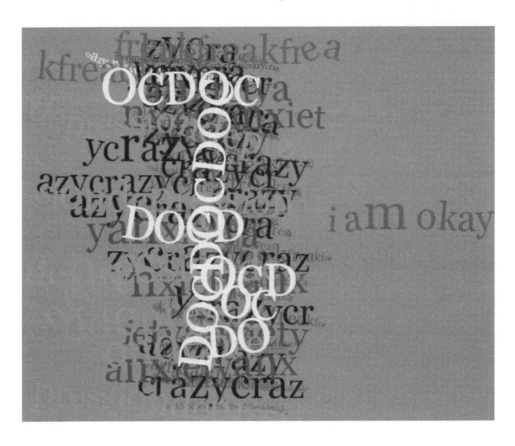

Part Two – Rinsing

Of my own making

How could the same thing
make and
unmake me?

Self-diagnosis

I didn't get a formal diagnosis.

All I know is that my arms gradually grew tired
from brushing out the knots in my hair.
I watched mutely
-    a bystander –
as clumps of my black tresses
plummeted to the ground after being yanked
from my head.
Every time
I finally remembered
to brush my hair.
Which wasn't very often.
At all.

I don't know if I was depressed or not.

I know that I became too tired to go
to the toilet more than twice
- sometimes once a day-
even when my lower back had a dull pain,
even when I woke up with a puffy face
(because of protein deposits
linked to urine retention).

I don't know if I was as depressed
as the characters they depict in movies and books.
I didn't feel as sadly pretty as they were.

All I know was that I suddenly
became constipated frequently.
Being too physically weak to push.

I don't remember if I was depressed or not.

I do remember glancing at my teeth
every other day.
Seeing them slowly turn an ugly yellow
(mimicking the dying yellow chrysanthemums
in my flower pot),
feeling them move slightly out of place
-    wobbling when my tongue pushed against them.
I didn't have the will to brush them

more than once a week maybe.

I don't think I am depressed.

Sometimes I am unable to
get into the shower at all.
Every day I make the resolve
and then forget for another week or so.
The shower-head looming frighteningly
-          its encased cascading waterfalls threatening
to submerge me entirely-
not long enough to strangle me,
but long enough to weaken me further.

I don't think I was depressed.

I sometimes didn't eat
more than once a day.
I was brutally forcing
the morsels down my throat
-sometimes for hours on end-
as though my body was
rejecting nourishment.

I don't think I am depressed.

But sometimes,
sometimes my throat is parched
from hours without hydration.
I cough and wheeze
and choke on air.
I still don't drink anything
(for a few more hours at least).

I don't think I am that depressed.

I feel like a child.
One that must learn to walk.
All over again.
Almost as though I have
forgotten how to.

Where do I begin?

How do I start to learn how to live?

Old things

I tried new things
but the carcass of the old things
took up too
much space

Deadly companion

Often my mind and I discuss you.
How time would be endless if you didn't exist,
how I would be different if you did not stealthily enter
through the backdoor of my hustled thoughts
and hide behind the curtains of my flaws.
Or if you had not totally burnt through
all my other traits and remained like the sole
firefly buzzing through a night sky
of dark thoughts.

Concentrating on your being when I am in
solitude and when I am
amidst the clobbering clownish crowds,
I find that you alone are my philosopher,
my friend, my enemy, my problem,
my strength, my weakness;
my sole constant companion.

Demolishing all bonds that bind me,
creating invisible impermeable boundaries
around me, I am caged
-    in here -
in this dark, infinite room with you
like a prisoner and a timid constantly
dripping tap.

Wounded

I started wearing gloves so that
the scars in my mind would be
hidden from the world,
along with the scars on my hands.

How was I to know that in doing so
I would simply be proclaiming it;
announcing that I was wounded
beyond repair.

Listening [to the heart]

Should I listen to you?
Should I listen to you once more?
You?
Of all people?
The most flawed,
most errant person I know.

I am in trouble again.
You are in trouble once more

You that cries when you should laugh;
that hurts when there are no wounds;
that cannot tell right from wrong.

The storm in my summer,
the smoke in my once cloudless eyes,
the ice in my winter voice,
the losing gambler in my casino of joy.

So full of hope,
potential,
yet afraid
of yourself.

So simple, plain
yet entangled
within yourself.

Should I trust you?

You apologise even before you falter.
You beg before you even try.
You whimper before the whip is even lifted.

Should I trust you?

Phobia

I don't think I was that afraid
of heights or germs or even
of intimacy.

I was afraid of the most probable,
likeliest, most commonplace thing
of all:
living.

Sleep eludes me

It is dark once more.
Night has fallen.
Yet, my eyes do not relent.

Memories flicker like lost fireflies.

Sleep is a forbidden intoxication.
I cannot trust the dark
-     it used to belong to me.

My mad, senseless confidante.
A silent friend singing praise of my strangeness.

It danced in every colour.
Resided within and around me.
Engulfed me like the sweet lullaby of the restless wind.
A wandering traveller,
a worthy companion.

An old lover.
A forgotten dream.

I run after it senselessly;
yearning for peace.

A colourless noise surrounds me.
The thread of sleep and peace
has mercilessly been broken.

The dark no longer rocks me gently to sleep;
its silence now pierces my calm mind like an intrusive dagger.

Dark cannot be trusted;
it has conspired with sleeplessness.

I wait for light.

When I think about writing about flowers

The world is falling apart. Tearing itself into pieces. Then breaking those pieces into tinier pieces. It's chewing itself up. Crunchingly. Crunch.

Chew.

Crunch.

Chew.

Spitting itself out. Vomiting. Convulsing.

Should I be writing about flowers at this time? Should I be getting lost in a garden? In a beautiful world of growth and beauty when war rages around me? Should I write about flowers when the weeds of negativity, of malice, of suspicion, of anger, of desolation are fed by the never-faltering winds of my pessimism? Carried on the backs of minute ants - too small to comprehend that the salty sugar pieces that they carry will create a sculpture of paranoia - of nervous frustration- in some abandoned corner of my mind. Should I be writing about flowers when the anxious caterpillars of my obsessions burrow into my hands – eating them from the inside-out, leaving behind beautiful wretched blood butterflies – bared, naked for all to see - to marvel, to mock:

my insanity; a kaleidoscope of my helpless, vulnerable, aggressive, disappointing scars.

Should I really be writing about flowers?

Hourglass

The days turned into weeks, the
weeks turned into months,
the months
into years.
I still felt
like
I
was
stuck.
I thought
time had been stuck
with me. That it was trapped
in an endless hourglass just like I was.

But when I finally looked up, time had changed everything.

E
    x
        c
            e
                p
                    t
                       me.

Quantifying an illness

254 days since I left my house.
At all.
255 days since I have pet my dogs.
619 days since I have given or received a hug.
2444 days since I watched a movie
At the cinema.
2460 days since I ate
in an actual restaurant.
2150 days since I have eaten takeout.
Pizza was the last, I think.
34 days since I have had a proper shower.
2 hours since I have washed my hands.
1.5 minutes since my last intrusive thought.

Hope(less)

Hope withered like a
changing tree in winter.

Not all at once
-     leaf by leaf-

silently.

Until one day nothing
was left
(except bare branches).

Under(stand)ing

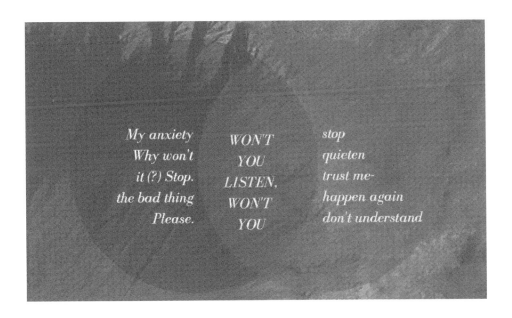

My anxiety   WON'T   stop
Why won't   YOU   quieten
it (?) Stop.   LISTEN,   trust me-
the bad thing   WON'T   happen again
Please.   YOU   don't understand

Into the light

I wanted to step into the light,
god knows some part of me
(really)
wanted to.

To bask in the sunshine.
To forget all that was dark and cold.

But the light seemed so unfamiliar.
I didn't know how to feel warmth anymore.

The invisible burden

"But you don't look ill",
they say.
As my body physically tires
-     rots away-
from the growing shadows;
feeding the fungus of
sickening thoughts in my mind.

"It'll go away someday",
"You just aren't trying hard enough",
they say.
I sure hope it will.
I try to catch my breath from playing
hide-and-seek from the thoughts
monopolising my time.

"Maybe you should take up a hobby",
they say.
Maybe I will.
When I get some time off
from washing my raw fingers.
Repeatedly.

"You don't look ill",
they say.
I show them my bleeding
-     sometimes deformed fingers.
They recoil in disgust and embarrassment.

"Do I look ill now?"

Attached

I wondered often:
is my disorder as attached to me
as I am to it?
Would it leave me
as easily as it had joined me?

Or would we have to live like this
forever?

Fragments of an incomplete whole;
misplaced harmony.

Squalor

The dirt has stuck onto the floor now.
Piles and piles of it.
Covering every inch of my once immaculate wooden floor.

There are scrunched-up kitchen towels and small pieces of paper
in corners.
The bin is overflowing
with used nitrile gloves and blood-stained tissues.

Used plastics lie on the table,
spilling onto the chair,
onto a mountain of clean laundry
that's been sitting there for months now.

Old Dettol bottles lie strewn in the lower right corner,
next to now empty glove cardboard boxes.

Six (maybe seven) pairs of shoes huddle together in the lower left corner.
Waiting.
Scared for when they'll get doused in disinfecting chemicals.

The leather chair
-worn out now-
-being the only place I can sit-
-being eroded from repetitive sanitizer burns-
has a polystyrene cup full of hot chocolate on its
seat.
The drink is probably cold now.

They all look on
-disapprovingly-
-dreadfully-
-sympathetically-
as I enter my twentieth minute of washing my hands.

A few drops of blood having been added to the pile of dirt stuck onto the floor.

Wash(ing)

It felt as though the agony was etched or stuffed under my skin.
I had to wash it.
Over and over again.
And again.
Until it left me.
Completely.

The skin left.
Sometimes the blood left.
But never the agony.

Failure

I see you laying there.
Face smashed into the cold tiled floor.
Your body
-    limb;
empty almost of all motion.
Your arms twitch a little.

I want to pick up you from the filthy floor; carry you to safety.
I know you trust me to do that.

But I cannot.

I feel frozen.

In shock.
In desperation.
In confusion.

I don't know how to pick up you.

Physically, I know I can.
Mentally, I know I cannot.

I haven't touched another person in months.
(I think I have forgotten how to).
I haven't held another body in years.
(I don't know how to).

Help comes eventually.

You're safe now.
Your head is bleeding somehow.

I can't do anything to help.
I stand in the furthest corner

Away from the mayhem,
Away from your blood.
Away from my failure.

From all the days I have lived with this disorder,
I think I hate this one the most.

Assurance

They told me to not wash my hands.
Now, everyone is washing theirs.

They told me that I shouldn't wear gloves so often.
So many are wearing them all the time now.

They told me to get used to hugging people
-to touching people-
-to shaking everyone's hands.
Now, there's a 6-foot distance between everyone.

They told me that I should go out more often.
Now everyone is locked up at home.

They told me that I should travel more
-stay in hotels more-
-eat take-out more.
Now, no-one can do any of those things.

Finally, they see the world as I do.
Finally, you see reality with the same distorted lens that I do.

Sometimes, the virus isn't only outside of us.
Sometimes, we don't only wash our hands
to keep our bodies clean.

The maybe maze

She left my medicine on the kitchen table.
She left my medicine in the same packaging that she bought it in.
The same packaging that everyone outside touched.
Maybe they sneezed on it.
Maybe they coughed on it.
Maybe they spoke over it.
Maybe they didn't wash their hands when they came
from the toilet before touching it.
She left my medicine on the table.
She left my medicine on the table next to another packet.
Maybe they sneezed on it.
Maybe they coughed on it.
Maybe they spoke over it.
Maybe they didn't wash their hands when they came
from the toilet before touching it.
I have to stretch over the table to get my medicine.
I have to stretch over the other packet on the table to get my medicine.
I have to stretch over their coughing.
I have to stretch over their sneezing.
I have to stretch over their talking.
I have to stretch over their touching.
Maybe I shouldn't take my medicine.
Maybe I should just wait.
Maybe.

Time

They say time heals
the deepest of wounds,
then how come the bruises
on my hands are darker now?
More than ever before.

Part Three– D(r)ying

Growth

I thought I would outgrow you.
I have outgrown everything.
Except for you.

If I ever

If I ever wonder within the realms of fantasy,

the sombreness of your voice

will beckon me back to reality.

If I ever get lost in the sheets of disillusionment,

the gentleness of your touch

will waken sleeping hope.

If I ever roam around helplessly in the endless maze

of life's predicaments, the exuberance

of your smile will brighten the dark road;

guiding me back home.

But if I ever forget you:

-who-

-what-

-where-

you are;

let the unsung hymn that you kindle in

the depths of your bosom

sing loudly to my silence.

For I

-being blinded by reality-

-spurned by fantasy-

will grope onto each

rhythm-less and clumsy note

and find my way back.

To you.

Fruits of the mind

She is no longer a ripe grape
but rather a wrinkled raisin
- a ghastly shadow -
holding only the seeds of her
fragmented life;
her wasted mind.

Endings

If I had known that endings would be
so endearing,
I would not have feared them
for most of my life.

If I had known that every tired, defeated
day would end with your gentle touch,
I would have braved on through the
seemingly endless days.

If I had known that all my uneven pathways
ended with your vivacious being and your
encompassing smile, I would have followed any
path
    -    no matter how crooked.

If I had known that the prayers
I've voiced in the depths of my
despair would touch my lips in the
form of yearning as soon as I laid eyes upon you,
I would have looked for divinity
in your being.
Only within your being.

Now, I am yours.

All of me.
Tired.
Defeated.
Worn.

I hand myself unto you.
Make me new.

Take these pieces of broken glass
and make an uncommon vase.
I will try not to cut you:
just please,
oh please
make me new.

Stuck

Here
-   in my small bubble of reality,
I tend to get a little obsessed:
I obsess over what I clean,
I obsess over what I buy,
I get stuck on cleaning what I buy
and buying what I cannot clean,
I obsess over what I cook,
I obsess over what I eat,
I eat what I cook and
I only cook how much I eat,
I obsess over how I clean when I cook,
I obsess over what I cook after I clean
-   the cycle of cleaning the gloves before I
wear them, cleaning my hands before I wash the
gloves, cleaning the gloves to wash the other
gloves before I wash my hands to wear the clean
gloves to clean the dirty gloves and you

-                    you   -

you were the first beautiful,
worthwhile thing that I got stuck on;
the thorns of your clarity,
-    stability -
piercing the bubble of isolation
I had surrounded myself in.

Your presence as simple and necessary
as the first rays of spring
-    falling on wilted tree branches,
saddened, frozen

in this never-ending
winter.

Disappointment

My life is not only mine.
I share it.
With all the other versions of myself that
I have disappointed.

Forgive [yourself]

Will you please look in my direction once more?

Not with eyes that pierce my confidence,
that mock my clumsiness,
but with a vision as pure as a white canvas that
looks upon my flaws
as a kaleidoscope.

Will you please speak to me once more?

My words are as jumbled as a scrabble board
knocked over by a child in playful irritation.
Please do not glue them together with
any ill intentions.

Speak to me with the caution of a thread sliding into the eye of a needle,
not with a double-sided sword that gashes mercilessly into my determination.

Will you hold me once more?

Not with the cold caress of an embittered wife,
but with the excited warmth of a first kiss.

Will you still love me, please?

Despite my countless flaws, clumsy actions,
miscalculated speech and tattered trust.

I am your stranger
- your own shadow-

oh please, will you please?

Butterfly

And just as the caterpillar
became a butterfly,
life didn't seem like a burden anymore.
It flew with small pretty wings.
Even if just for a short while.

Refugee

I hide from the darkness of the world,
trying to find some comfort between the
letters that I memorize.
Words of affirmation.
Words that make me feel normal.
Less strange at the least.

I embrace the sterility of the walls inside,
sheltering myself from the rainbow of outside.

I tune into the white noise inside,
having grown tired of their sensationalistic music.

I lay covered by my cold,
hiding from their warmth.

I am struggling to breathe now.

My own air suffocating me.
My own coldness burning me.
My own noise bleeding through my ears.
My own letters mocking me for my strangeness.

I open the doors.
I open my doors.
To the outside.
To their outside.
To them.

I have been rejected
-left desolate-
-rendered homeless-
by myself.

I am now their refugee.

In every intrusive thought, there is a memory

In every intrusive thought, there is a memory.
In every memory, there is a mishap.
In every mishap, there is a victim.
In every victim, there is a sense of self-blame.
In every sense of self-blame, there is a lack of self-confidence.
In every lack of self-confidence, there is a questioning of morality.
In every questioning of morality, there is a sense of not being the victim.
In every sense of not being the victim, there is another mishap.
In every mishap, there is a memory.
In every memory, there is an intrusive thought

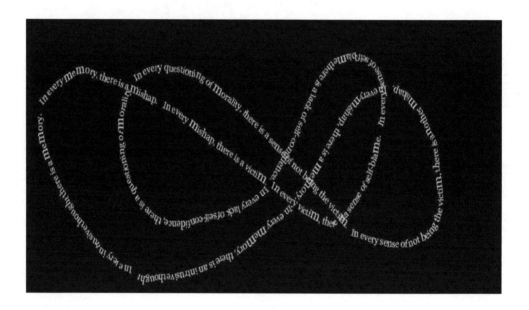

Crumbs

And it dawned on me suddenly:
I didn't know how to live.
I didn't know how to eat.
I didn't know how to sleep properly
or even how to use the bathroom normally.

It's like this disorder had systematically hollowed
out my personality.
Eroding and rusting
all my likes and dislikes
-          leaving behind only remnants,

crumbs.

Somehow,
I had to make a meal
-food-
-sustenance-
-life-

from these
crumbs.

On some days, I have killed myself at least twice before breakfast

Metaphorically, everyone should kill themselves at least once. It helps dispel the gnawing bugs of suicidal thoughts that feast on my negativity. On some days, I have killed myself at least twice before breakfast.

I have killed my vices. Some have died; some have been promptly reborn. Sometimes, I have killed some of my virtues. Virtues sometimes sting just as painfully as vices do - if captured by the wrong vessel. I have strangled desires, slowly watching them suffocate till they drown. I have shot down goals, aspirations, weaknesses. I have weeded out some pain from my ever-growing garden of wild emotion. I have washed myself away - almost daily and have remoulded my personality. Sometimes, it grows back just the same. Sometimes, it grows back a little mis-shapen, a little disfigured, a little mutilated. It grows back, nonetheless.

I am eternal. I am insoluble. I can't be burnt with fire, nor drowned with water. I am immortal.

We are immortal.

Sandstorm

a small

sandstorm

some ominous dance

something
to do with you.
Something inside of you.
step

right inside

step by step.

white sand
like

swirling
pulverized bones.

violent,
symbolic

thousand razor

blades

Under lock and key

I don't want to talk about my problems; I don't want to discuss it with anyone. If I do, what if they don't understand – misunderstand? Put the pieces of the broken vase back together in the wrong way: the jagged pieces slicing into the tender flesh of the unaware holder. Their blood smearing their fingers, dropping to the floor; everything scattered. All over again.

What if they think I am a freak? What if they lock me up and throw away the key? What if no one can hear my screams echoing through the shut doors, through the sterile walls - mingled with all the other screams of insanity? The yelps of destitution, the pleas of the misunderstood, the misconstrued, the *demonised*.

What if my pleas for help get lost in the sea of all the other despaired yelps? Rivers of incomprehensible shouts rushing to merge into one consuming never-ending ocean of pain- waves of sanity sporadically hitting against the rocks of normalcy.

What if I am made to live inside another prison? A prison outside of my mind. A prison I can't recognise. A prison I can't wash away.

Difficult (re)introductions

A tinge ever so golden
laughing at the corner of her eyes,
now forgotten.
But oh, the black rings
were ever so swollen,
like a sweater
in ill faith begotten.

Sleep healthily she must not.
Alas, her brain will rot.

Scrubbing clean floors
till the crack of dawn,
she almost started cleaning the door
-         save her energy was drawn.

Burn marks on her forehead and chin
deliberately placed
there as though to punish for some sin.

Harmful chemicals on her skin did she place,
she didn't even spare her face!

Dimples and smile lines
eroded by the sands of troubles ever so fine.

Stinging of my raw and cracked hands,
back into harsh reality do I land.
Curiosity to meet this girl
prompts me to say at will:
'Hello',
I say.

Across the mirror, gold sparks play.
Introduce me to me,

like old days,
like how I used to be.

Ghosts

I heard a sound;
a slight whimper.

Was it coming from the window?
It was definitely glass but it was not
coming from the window.

I saw it:
it was grey.

It floated just above the floor
but wait
-         it had a face just like mine.

Instead of my downtrodden moist eyes,
it had sparkly excited, smiling eyes.
In place of my frown, there was
a grinning giggly mouth

Her bare hands were displayed against the glass,
in arrogance of my scarred,
glove-covered ones.
She was mocking
my pitiable state.

The sound was not coming from the window;
it was coming from the mirror.

I was being haunted by a ghost.

The ghost of who I once was.
The ghost of me.

The gift of insanity

The rope ceases to hold me;
the burden of a questioning mind
is too cumbersome for it.

Falling into an abyss
of paradoxical thinking,
moral quagmires
and unfinished
endings,
I grope onto this
simple cotton thread.

The thread that stitches together all my
flaws and misunderstood emotions,
keeping me whole on the inside;
but wholly broken, fully incomplete on
the outside
-           screeching for rescue.

This thread is simple.
This thread is thin.
This thread is the fine line
between the dead and the undead,
the sane and the insane;

the only feeling that reminds me
that I am
still indeed
here.

Still alive.

Dear Childhood

Come back.
Take me back
to a time where
the nudity of my thoughts
weren't embraced in the cloak
of disturbed age.

Come back.
Take me back
to a time where
I didn't tightrope walk
on the boundaries of
normalcy,
breathe within the restraints
of my mind.

Come back.
Take me back
to a time where
I could weave dreams,
freely.
Under the shade of trees,
thinking that I was,
 I am,
unimaginably
limitless.

Shiksha Dheda is a South African of Indian descent. She uses writing to express her OCD and depression roller-coaster ventures. Sometimes, she dabbles in photography, painting, and baking lopsided layered cakes.

Her writing has been featured(on/forthcoming) in Brittle Paper, Door is a jar, Luna Luna Mag and Versification, amongst others.

This is her debut poetry collection.

She rambles annoyingly at Twitter: @ShikshaWrites. You can find (or ignore her) at https://shikshadheda.wixsite.com/writing/poetry,

1) *Is the door locked?* published in Brave Voices Magazine, January 2021
2) *Home* published in Versification Zine Medicated Mic issue, March 2021
3) *Fruits of the tree* published in Selcouth Station, July 2021
4) *Shadow* forthcoming in Ninshar Arts
5) *Gone Fishing* forthcoming in Ninshar Arts
6) *Heart(less)* published in Dead Fern Press, January 2021.
7) *The find* published in Ghost Heart Literary Journal, March 2021
8) *The warrior* published in Fat Cat Magazine, March 2021
9) *Fungi* published in Hencroft Hub Issue 1, April 2021
10) *I am okay* published in Petrichor Magazine Issue 17, April 2021
11) *Self-diagnosis* published in Anti-Heroin Chic Issue 20, April 2021
12) *Old Things* published in Fevers of the Mind, February 2021
13) *Deadly Companion* published in Poetically Mag, April 2021
14) *Listening[to the heart]* published in Fevers of the Mind, August 2021
15) *Phobia* forthcoming in Ninshar Arts
16) *When I think about writing about flowers* published in Paranoid Tree, Vol 8, June 2021
17) *Hourglass* published in The Global Youth Review Issue II, June 2021
18) *Quantifying an illness* published in Neurological Literary Magazine, January 2021. Re-printed in The Global Youth Review Issue II, June 2021
19) *Hope (less)* forthcoming in Farther Trees
20) *Under(stand)ing* published in Selcouth Station, July 2021
21) *The Invisible Burden* published in Fahmidan Journal Issue 6, May 2021
22) *Squalor* published in Capsule Stories Second Isolation Edition, July 2021
23) *Wash(ing)* published in Casino Literary Magazine Second Volume, August 2021
24) *Failure* published in Off Menu Press Memory Edition, March 2021
25) *The maybe maze* published in Mixed Mag Issue 6, February 2021.
26) *Growth* published in Dead Fern Press, January 2021
27) *If I ever* published in Fevers of the Mind, February 2021
28) *Disappointment* published in Glitchwords Issue 5, April 2021
29) *Refugee* published in Visual Verse Vol 08 Chapter 03, January 2021
30) *In every intrusive thought, there is a memory* published in Streetcake Magazine, Issue 74.1, August 2021
31) *Crumbs* published in The Kalahari Review, March 2021
32) *On some days, I have killed myself at least twice before* breakfast published in 3Moon Magazine Issue 7, May 2021
33) *Sandstorm* published in Hooligan Mag, March 2021
34) *Difficult (re)introductions* published in Small Leaf Press Jaden Issue 1, April 2021

Manufactured by Amazon.ca
Bolton, ON